SHUT THE FUCK UP AND JUST DO IT

UNCENSORED ADVICE FOR A NO-BULLSHIT LIFE

LAINE CUNNINGHAM

Shut the Fuck Up and Just Do It
Uncensored Advice for a No-Bullshit Life

Published by Sun Dogs Creations
Changing the World One Book at a Time

Cover Design by Angel Leya

Copyright © 2018 Laine Cunningham

All rights reserved. No part of this book may be reproduced in any form or by any means, electronic, mechanical, digital, photocopying or recording, except for the inclusion in a review, without permission in writing from the publisher.

ISBN: 9781946732743

Dedicated to my no-bullshit friend
and a fucking awesome guy
Rich Ehisen

PULL WHATEVER THE HELL
FLEW UP YOUR ASS
OUT OF YOUR ASS,
ALL RIGHT?

THE SOONER YOU REALIZE THAT
THE GOOD OLD DAYS ARE A LIE
PERPETUATED BY WASHED-UP FUCKS
WHO WANT YOU TO FEEL INFERIOR,
THE SOONER YOU CAN APPRECIATE
WHAT'S RIGHT IN FRONT OF YOU.

ARE YOU REALLY
SUCH A RAGING DICK
THAT YOU ACTUALLY HAVE
NO FUCKING CLUE?

NO ONE EVER CHANGED THE WORLD
BEING CODDLED BY THEIR NANNY, SO
TOUGHEN THE FUCK UP.

OH, THAT'S NOT FAIR? WELL,
LIFE DOESN'T HAVE A
FUCKING PLAYGROUND MONITOR.

STOP BUNCHING YOUR PANTIES
INTO A GODDAMN WAD AND
LISTEN.

EVERYTHING GOOD IS
WORTH THE EFFORT, SO
GET OFF YOUR ASS AND
PUT IN THE FUCKING EFFORT.

NO SECRET SOCIETIES OR
GRAND CONSPIRACIES ARE
PINNING YOU DOWN.
LIFE IS HARD.
GET FUCKING USED TO IT.

THINGS COULD BE A LOT WORSE, SO
SHUT THE FUCK UP AND BE GRATEFUL
FOR ONCE IN YOUR MISERABLE LIFE.

IF YOU DON'T LIKE IT, FOR GOD'S SAKE,
QUIT FUCKING MOANING ABOUT IT AND
GET OFF YOUR ASS AND CHANGE IT.

STOP SWINGING YOUR DICK.
IT'S REALLY NOT THAT BIG
TO BEGIN WITH.

HERE'S AN IDEA: WHY DON'T YOU
TRY SAYING "THANK YOU"
ONCE IN A FUCKING WHILE?

NO GIANT ASSHOLE NEEDS TO DIE
FOR YOU TO RISE TO THE TOP.
YOUR ASS ALREADY COMMANDS
ALL THE AUTHORITY
YOU WILL EVER NEED.

PERFECTION IS A LIE, SO
QUIT FUCKING NITPICKING AND
LEAVE EVERYONE THE FUCK ALONE.

SOMETIMES SHIT JUST HAPPENS,
SO QUIT BLAMING EVERYONE ELSE AND
SHOVEL THE SHIT YOUR GODDAMN SELF.

NO ONE "DESERVES" ANYTHING,
SO QUIT FUCKING WHINING
ABOUT ALL THE MEAN PEOPLE
IN YOUR MISERABLE FUCKING LIFE.

GET OFF YOUR GODDAMN PONY,
TAKE OFF THAT STUPID PARTY HAT, AND
JOIN THE REAL FUCKING WORLD.

STOP DELIBERATELY FUCKING UP
THE GOOD SHIT OTHER PEOPLE
TRY TO DO FOR YOU.

HOW STUPID DO YOU HAVE TO BE
TO THINK THE WORLD WILL RECOGNIZE
YOUR AWESOME MAGNIFICENCE,
YOU FUCKING INSIGNIFICANT FLEA?

PICK YOU SORRY, DROOPING ASS
OFF THE GODDAMN FLOOR AND
JOLLY THE FUCK UP ALREADY.

WOULD YOU JUST STOP
FOR ONE GODDAMN MINUTE AND
LISTEN TO THE SHIT THAT
COMES OUT OF YOUR MOUTH?

WHEN LIFE HANDS YOU LEMONS,
PUCKER THE FUCK UP BECAUSE
ONLY LOSERS THINK THEY
ARE SUPPOSED TO WIN.

HEY! ASSHOLE!
NO ONE HAS TO AGREE WITH YOU, SO
STOP BEING A DICK ABOUT IT.

YOU WILL NEVER FIND A THRONE
BUILT ESPECIALLY FOR YOUR ASS, SO
QUIT ACTING LIKE ROYALTY
AND WISE THE FUCK UP.

ARE YOU FOR FUCKING REAL, OR
DID I JUST DROP INTO THE ALTERNATE UNIVERSE
WITH EVIL KIRK?

YOU'RE NOT AS FUCKING WONDERFUL
AS YOU SEEM TO THINK, SO
TRY SOME FUCKING KINDNESS
NOW AND THEN.

STOP ACTING LIKE
SOMEONE SHOULD THROW YOU A PARTY
EVERY GODDAMN DAY AND
DO IT YOUR FUCKING SELF.

FOR FUCK'S SAKE, TAKE OFF
THAT SHIT-SMEARED DIAPER AND
ACT LIKE A FUCKING ADULT.

NO ONE CARES HOW MANY
PARTICIPATION AWARDS YOU GOT
AS A CHILD. YOU'RE NOT A FUCKING CHILD,
AND YOU'RE NOT GETTING ANOTHER
LAME-ASS PARTICIPATION AWARD.
EVER.

NOBODY LIKES A JACKASS,
LEAST OF ALL A JACKASS
WITH AN ATTITUDE
LIKE YOURS,
JACKASS.

NO ONE APPRECIATES
SELF-RIGHTEOUS ASSHOLES, SO
CUT THE FUCKING PURITAN ACT,
WOULD YOU?

IT SUCKS THAT YOU WERE BULLIED
AS A CHILD, BUT BULLIES DON'T
MAGICALLY VAPORIZE WHEN
THEY TURN EIGHTEEN, SO
GROW SOME FUCKING BALLS.

QUIT BEING SO FUCKING SQUEAMISH
ABOUT TAKING RESPONSIBILITY AND
GET THE HELL ON WITH YOUR LIFE.

NOBODY WANTS TO BE NEAR
AN ASSHOLE,
ESPECIALLY NOT AN ASSHOLE
THAT EXPELS AS MUCH SHIT
AS YOU DO.

IF YOU DON'T
WISE THE FUCK UP,
YOU ARE GOING TO DIE
FROM FUCKING STUPIDITY.

I'M NOT YOUR FUCKING PARENT, AND NEITHER IS YOUR FUCKING BOSS. DEAL WITH IT.

HEY, PAL! IN LOVE, SUCCESS,
AND PRETTY MUCH ALL OF LIFE
YOU HAVE TO GIVE TWO SHITS
ABOUT SOMEONE
OTHER THAN YOURSELF.

NOBODY GIVES A SHIT ABOUT YOUR MONEY OR
YOUR PISSANT LUXURY LIFESTYLE, SO
KEEP THE TESLA, THE YACHT, AND THE
GILDED NOSEPICKER TO YOURSELF.

HEY! I'M NOT YOUR
FUCKING THERAPIST, SO
TURN THE DRAMA DOWN
ONE GODDAMN NOTCH!

WHY DON'T YOU TRY
UNCORKING YOUR THUMB
FROM YOUR ASS AND
GIVE ME A CALL WHEN YOU
ACTUALLY HAVE YOUR SHIT TOGETHER?

SO SORRY, BUT YOU'RE NOT
THE FRESH FLAVOR OF THE DAY.
QUIT FUCKING ACTING LIKE YOU ARE.

LOVE IS A MANY SPLENDORED THING, BUT
YOU'VE TAKEN THIS LONG TO
REACH MEDIOCRE, SO
GET IT THE FUCK IN GEAR.

SORRY, DUDE.
LIFE DOESN'T COME WITH
TRIGGER WARNINGS.
TRY SOME FUCKING THERAPY.

HEY, DIPSHIT!
THE DAY YOU WERE BORN,
THE WORLD DID NOT
FALL TO ITS FUCKING KNEES, AND
IT'S NOT ABOUT TO NOW.

WHY DON'T YOU DIAL DOWN THAT
CONTROLLING ASSHOLE SHIT AND
GIVE PEOPLE
HALF A FUCKING CHANCE?

INSTEAD OF PROCLAIMING
HOW GREAT YOU ARE, STEP
THE FUCK ASIDE AND LET PEOPLE
WHO ACTUALLY KNOW WHAT THEY'RE DOING
TAKE THE FUCKING LEAD.

GUESS WHAT? THE PLANET WILL KEEP SPINNING AFTER YOU DIE, SO TRY NOT TO THINK OF YOURSELF AS SUCH A HOT PILE OF SHIT.

QUIT FUCKING TALKING AND
START FUCKING DOING.

INSTEAD OF BORING EVERYONE
WITH YOUR LAME-ASS IDEAS
ABOUT YOUR LAME-ASS LIFE,
SHUT THE FUCK UP AND
JUST DO IT.

NOVELS BY LAINE CUNNINGHAM

The Family Made of Dust
Beloved
Reparation

OTHER BOOKS BY LAINE CUNNINGHAM

Woman Alone
A Six-Month Journey Through the Australian Outback

On the Wallaby Track
Essential Australian Words and Phrases

Seven Sisters
Spiritual Messages from Aboriginal Australia

Writing While Female or Black or Gay
Diverse Voices in Publishing

The Zen of Travel
The Zen of Gardening
Zen in the Stable
The Zen of Chocolate
The Zen of Dogs
The Wisdom of Puppies
The Wisdom of Babies
The Wisdom of Weddings

Travel Photo Art Series

Bikes of Berlin
Necropolises of New Orleans I & II
Ruins of Rome I & II
Ancients of Assisi I & II
Panoramas of Portugal
Nuances of New York
Utopia of the Unicorn

www.ingramcontent.com/pod-product-compliance
Lightning Source LLC
Chambersburg PA
CBHW071545080526
44588CB00011B/1803